WHAT IF YOU HAD

Animal Eyes!?

Sandra Markle

Illustrated by
Howard McWilliam

Scholastic Inc.

For Janie Hachen
and the children
at Cottonwood
Elementary in
Andover, Kansas

A special thank-you to Skip Jeffery for his loving support
during the creative process.

Photos ©: 4: Hiroya Minakuchi/Minden Pictures/Getty Images; 7 inset: Nature
Picture Library/Superstock, Inc.; 8: Pobytov/Getty Images; 11 inset: Joel Sartore/
National Geographic Photo Ark; 13 inset: FLPA/Treat Davidson/age fotostock;
14: Worldfoto/Dreamstime; 15 inset: William Jr/Getty Images; 16: Picture by
Tambako the Jaguar/Getty Images; 17 inset: Richard Du Toit/Minden Pictures/
Getty Images; 18: BluePlanetArchive/Kat Bolstad; 19 inset: Norbert Wu/Minden
Pictures/Getty Images; 20: Owen Franken/Getty Images; 21 inset: Pablo Hidalgo/
Dreamstime; 23 inset: Ivkuzmin/Dreamstime; 24: Ken Yoshida/Getty Images;
25 inset: Vitaly Titov/Dreamstime. All other photos © Shutterstock.com.

What if one day, you woke up with
a wild animal's eyes instead of your own?

CHAMELEON

Chameleon eyes are tricky.
Each eye can move separately.
That way, it can look around
in two directions at once.

So, it quickly spots bugs.
ZAP! Time to eat.

With chameleon eyes, you'd scan fast. You would find what you want in a flash!

FACT

Its cone-shaped eyes are fused-together eyelids.

GOLDEN EAGLE

Golden eagle eyes have super sight.
This bird can spot a rabbit two miles away.
It stays focused on its prey until it catches dinner.

With golden eagle eyes, you'd see GREAT. You could watch games from high-up seats.

FACT

Eagle eyes have a third eyelid that cleans the eyes like windshield wipers.

DRAGONFLY

Dragonfly eyes are huge!
Each has up to 310,000 lenses.
That is how it quickly sees something move.
So, it spots flying bugs in time to
catch and eat them!

With dragonfly eyes, you'd be a star reporter. You'd see everything that is happening.

FACT

Three extra eyes guide its flight path. So, dragonflies fly without crashing.

9

CLOUDED LEOPARD

Clouded leopard eyes have a mirrorlike layer. It bounces light back through the retina (ret-uh-nuh). That layer has light-sensing cells for sight. So, bounced light helps the cat see at night. And it makes its eyes seem to glow.

With clouded leopard eyes, dark places won't scare you.

FACT

At night, its *pupils* (pyoo-puhlz) open 100 times bigger to let in more light.

BULLFROG

A bullfrog's eyes are on top of its head.
It can hide underwater and peek out.
That's how it stays safe from birds.
And how it finds bugs to catch.
Its eyes also sink as it swallows.
That helps push food down its throat!

With bullfrog eyes, you'd blink to swallow. BIG bites? No problem!

FACT

Frogs have extra, see-through eyelids. Built-in swim goggles!

FOUR-EYED FISH

A four-eyed fish has only two eyes.
But each has two different parts.
It swims with just the top part above the water
to watch for birds after a fish dinner.
The bottom part looks underwater for the bugs
or tiny fish it eats.

With four-eyed fish eyes, you could bike and read at the same time. Watch where you're going!

FACT

Four-eyed fish swim in groups. Lots of eyes always watching!

YELLOW MONGOOSE

Yellow mongoose pupils are rectangles (rek-*tang*-guhl). This gives it a very wide view. When it sees bugs or lizards, it catches them to eat. If it spots an enemy, it runs away FAST!

With yellow mongoose eyes, you'd ace laser tag.

FACT

To see far away,
a yellow mongoose stands tall.

17

COLOSSAL
SQUID

Colossal squid eyes are GIANT!
Each is as big as a soccer ball.
A part at the back produces light.
It is like having eyes with flashlights.
That is just what a colossal squid needs.
Its home down deep in the ocean is dark.

With colossal squid eyes, you could easily go for nighttime hikes!

FACT

Giant squid have BIG eyes, too.
But its eyes can't glow.

giant squid

LLAMA

A llama's eyes have special crystals. In bright sun, they form dark bands across its pupils. These become built-in llama sunglasses.

With llama eyes, you'd never squint while in the spotlight.

FACT

Llama eyelashes are sunshades, too.

DESERT
HORNED VIPER

Desert horned viper eyelids are clear.
They are also always sealed shut.
That makes them viper safety goggles.

With horned viper eyes, NO goggles are needed! You could do experiments safely.

FACT

This snake regularly sheds its skin. Its new skin includes new eyelids!

23

TARSIER

A tarsier (tahr-see-ur) has GIANT eyes. Its pupils close pinpoint small in bright light. But they open BIG in the dark. No wonder a tarsier is a great nighttime bug hunter.

With tarsier eyes, day and night, you would throw all base stealers OUT!

FACT

Each tarsier eye weighs more than its brain.

What if you could keep wild animal eyes?

Which animal eyes would be right for you?

Luckily, you don't have to choose.
Your eyes will always be people eyes.

They are just what you need to read,
to look around and discover,
and to see the people you love!

HOW YOUR EYES WORK

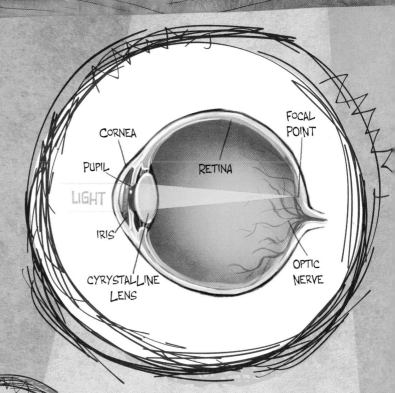

CORNEA

FOCAL POINT

PUPIL

RETINA

LIGHT

IRIS

CYRYSTALLINE LENS

OPTIC NERVE

Light enters through your pupils. It passes through lenses and a clear jelly. At the back, light strikes the retina. That sends signals to your brain. Then you SEE!

KEEP YOUR
EYES HEALTHY

- Don't let anything touch your eyes.
- If needed, wear glasses to help you see better.
- Wear safety goggles as needed.
- Always wear sunglasses when it is sunny.
- See your family eye doctor for checkups.

OTHER BOOKS IN THE SERIES